MORE 'TALK TIDY'

*Further to
the art of speaking
Wenglish*

By

John E

2003

TIDYPRINT PUBLICATIONS

CREIGIAU

© 2003 Tidyprint Publications

ISBN 0-9546659-1-0

Dedication

This one is for all my nearest and dearest -
Mair, Gareth, and Jane

This new edition first published by
Tidyprint Publications, 2003

First published by D. Brown & Sons Ltd, 1986

This edition printed by
Chas Hunt & Company (Cardiff) Ltd

Distributed by Welsh Books Council
Unit 16, Glanyrafon Enterprise Park, Llanbadarn, Aberystwyth, Ceredigion SY23 3AQ
Tel: 01970 624455
e-mail: www.cllc.org.uk

Illustrations by *Gren*

FOREWORD

Almost twenty years have elapsed since *Talk Tidy* was first published, so it is with some sense of disbelief that the reissued books are commended.

I am much indebted to Don Llewellyn and Brian Wood for their enthusiastic encouragement; and particularly to Brian, who has shown great skill, tenacity, and patience in ensuring success to the enterprise.

Sincere thanks are expressed to Gren; I count it a great privilege that this incomparable artist has decided to contribute.

John Edwards

December 2003

Introduction

Reactions to *Talk Tidy* – the book, the cassettes, and the CDs, – have been overwhelming in terms of warmth, pleasure, and positive response to what was offered. I am truly grateful to the many people – from local parts and from very much further afield – who took the trouble to write, to 'phone, and to relay messages at second and third hand. Their comments and suggestions for a further book (whose publication was taken for granted by them, but not by me) are gratefully acknowledged.

There can be no doubt that a major element in the response to Talk Tidy was nostalgia. So many people told me of pleasant memories of childhood and of days of their youth being stirred as they recalled older relatives 'who used to speak exactly like that.' More than one correspondent reminisced of days when 'ducking-apple night' evoked more pleasant memories than the current vogue for 'trick-or-treat' on *'Nos Cyn Gaeaf'* (the Welsh for 'Hallowe'en', which literally means 'Night Before Winter'). Days when local children actually played games like 'strong-horse-weak-donkeys' were recalled in truly vivid detail.

It would require a separate book to list all the memories which Talk Tidy seems to have stirred, but those which were recalled most frequently are the Jazz Band contests of the twenties and thirties, Sunday School outings to Barry Island and Porthcawl, church and chapel activities like Band of Hope, Christian Endeavour, Cymanfaoedd Ganu (Singing Festivals), 'tea-fights' at Christmas and other seasons in chapel, and Sunday School anniversary events.

Secular events were mentioned frequently, especially the 'drama-weeks' in Workmen's Halls, operettas, cantatas, carnivals, and other events in the local parks like rugby and football (cricket was mentioned only once, whilst bowls and tennis received not a single mention). The language which was associated with children's pursuits received especial mention and it is apparent that a rich linguistic variety was discernible since every local area seems to have had its own special words for these games.

There appear to have been Wenglish words and phrases used for almost all childhood games like 'Whip and Top', 'Bowleys/Bowlies', 'Catty and Doggy,' 'Photos', Marbles (these games alone produced so many words, mostly local in their currency, to describe the different types of marbles and the various techniques used in their operation, that a glossary for these alone would be needed), 'Mob', 'Dickie Show Your Light', 'Whistle, Speak or Hollo/Holler', 'Dickie Five Stones', 'Dip-Dap-Doh', and all the marvellous variations of language in games like 'Scotch' and the rich variety of skipping games.

One lady who recalled many vivid details in her letter also said, 'How about "Walk Tidy" for the title to your next book? Dealing with the habits and customs of the valleys' communities, I remember being told to "walk tidy!" by my mother when, dressed in "Sunday Best", I kicked a stone on the road on my way to chapel.'

Most gratifying to me, without doubt, was the trouble taken by so many people to show how warmly they endorse my assertion that Wenglish is 'the authentic voice of Anglo-Welshness in large areas of South Wales, is the oral badge of identity for many who live there, and a vital element in their social heritage.' No author can remain unmoved when reading words like the following in a letter from an Ynysybwl man 'exiled' in Welsh-speaking West Wales: 'Thank you for your book and cassette which, for all the humour, have dignified the language and lives of the valleys ... I'm grateful to you for showing that there's a vigour, an inheritance, a wit and culture which we products of the South Wales valleys can celebrate ...'

This, and other messages confirm me in the view that the prime purpose of writing *Talk Tidy,* and in recording its accompanying cassette with that most responsive and delightful audience at Aberdare, was to celebrate the continued existence of Wenglish. I cherish, too, the many messages from those who told me, 'Yes, we do talk like that – we do use those words, and now, thanks to you, we have a better understanding about *why* we use them.'

The Welsh are great colonisers and the current geographical location of Welsh exiles is simply mind-boggling. It would require much space to record all the countries to which copies of the *Talk Tidy* material have found their way. When one is sure that every obviously inhabited area of the world has been covered, along comes a message to say that *this* book or *this* tape is destined for a country which has been left out of the reckoning. A letter from Holland is recalled for a number of pleasant reasons, but chiefly because the local exile expressed warm thanks for confirmation in 'black and white' of the existence of the word 'scrammed' as Wenglish for 'scratched'. He now had proof, he said, for sceptical acquaintances who had long since doubted his word.

Although people from days long ago are inevitably recalled by the speech patterns recorded in *Talk Tidy,* it must *not* be thought that Wenglish is simply 'talk of yester-year'. The response from young people has both surprised and delighted me, since, at no time did I think of the material as having any real appeal to anyone who had yet to attain his thirtieth or fortieth birthday. How wrong can you be? 'Delight' is the word which best seems to sum up the younger element's reaction. I took only a marginal interest in a newspaper account of some research which had been undertaken in a university college in England which I read about some months ago. This seemed to show that, far from becoming uniform speakers of standard English, today's young people are both showing great interest in, and also using traditional, dialectic speech forms. In my own more modest fashion, I have received ample proof from young people that the researcher's conclusions seem to be founded in fact.

No small satisfaction has been gained from learning that in a number of Mid Glamorgan schools, both English and Welsh-medium, the Talk Tidy material is being used for teaching purposes. If this can be another means of helping pupils to take pride in acceptable local speech forms and to understand when non-regional, standard forms of speech are required for effective communication, particularly in interviews and when speaking to those who are not locals, then pupils will be more adequately prepared for adult life.

Although no longer actively engaged in the state education system, I continue to take delight in talking to youngsters locally and further afield. The use of Wenglish is very much a feature of the speech of young folk in the valleys' communities, and those who assert that Wenglish is merely an archaic lingo are undoubtedly wrong. It has to be asked, 'How well are they *listening* to the speech which continues to surround them?'

When pressed to supply evidence to support my contention that Wenglish is still spoken hereabouts by all age-groups, I always offer the following account of a true incident which occurred within the last few months. My wife and I enjoy looking after a young Border Collie bitch, Sally, who belongs to our son and daughter-in-law. One day, whilst standing in the garden with Sally, I heard the familiar, local expression used to attract the attention of dogs – 'Ee-ya boy!' Our neighbour's grandsons, then aged eight and six respectively, were peering over the wall and calling to Sally. 'Ee-ya boy!' repeated the younger lad. The older boy's rejoinder to his brother contained all the scorn that only an older brother can employ when putting younger ones to right: 'Use youer eyes, carn yue,' he said, 'bitch she is, mun!' All that needs to be added is that, whilst the boys' mother is a local girl, Dad is a Scot.

A final word, please, on reactions to Talk Tidy. The reviews of the book and tape in local and regional papers and in a number of worthy journals have been unvaryingly supportive and balanced. I am grateful for the positive and constructive criticism which was offered. One such reviewer, having mentioned the delight which Welsh schoolchildren show in their response to stories about Lancashire school pupils, proceeds to say that what is needed is 'a South Walian Bill Naughton who will dignify the lives of ordinary valley children' – how right he is!

Although Wenglish is not really a dialect of English and has never been afforded the respect which other regional dialects enjoy, the warmth, vitality, colour, and texture of our local speech need to be captured by a Wenglish author to ensure that the unique patterns and rhythms are more widely appreciated. I have long since held the opinion that a definitive play* about life 'round 'ere using authentic local speech presented in a way which people elsewhere can understand, will accomplish a great deal in the matter of ensuring an acceptable status for Wenglish.

The same kindly critic continues by saying of me '... ultimately, he is helping to restore the dignity and self-esteem of communities whose identities are threatened economically, socially, and culturally.' It must be said that, at no time, did I view my efforts in this high light. If however, Talk Tidy and More Talk Tidy (I hope) contribute in some small measure to restore much-needed dignity and self-esteem to valley communities, then I am more than delighted.

John Edwards

Abercynon
October 1986

*Footnote

As though in answer to a prayer, since the foregoing was written, several plays have been performed which give long-overdue recognition to the status of our 'oral badge of identity'. For as long as such staunch champions of the language as Rhondda dramatist Frank Vickery and others continue to write, so will our beloved Wenglish endure.

Abercynon, December 2003

The Pronunciation of Wenglish

It has been most gratifying to hear from many people, not locally born and 'rared', who have settled in our midst – those whom I like to call 'foreigners with a small 'f''. I have been delighted by their response, which largely is that of expressing gratitude for the insight provided into Wenglish and its development. The majority have asked for further guidance on the pronunciation of Wenglish so that they may not only understand better but be able more effectively to respond, i.e. to 'talk *more* tidy'.

A tape can obviously offer greatest help in this context but some outline guidance, particularly on the distinctive vowel sounds in Wenglish, is offered here. In spite of the purists' obsession with the slovenly aspects of Wenglish, it must be said that the vowel sounds heard in these parts, unlike the strangulated and affected vowel sounds which are encountered in Received Pronunciation ('refined cockney') are reasonably pure and un-adulterated.

A The following sentence shows the 'a' vowel at work in Wenglish: 'Mabel said she'd been bad (ill) but after she'd had her bath she'd be able to take a half of lager.' All the 'a' sounds are long, except for 'after' which is abbreviated to the point of being somewhat clipped. It should be noted that a pure Wenglish 'a' sound is used in both 'Mabel' and 'able'; these, also sable, gable, table, fable etc. are not to be pronounced as in Received Pronunciation, i.e. as 'Mayble', ayble', 'tayble', etc.

E and I Since these vowel sounds differ very little in Wenglish usage from the sounds encountered in other acceptable English usages, they present little or no difficulty to the learner. It should be noted, however, that 'ear' and 'year' are pronounced locally as though both were spelled 'year'.

O This sentence offers guidance on the use made of the letter 'o'; 'That shop over by there is 'opeluss' cos only one hour it's opun.' 'Shop' and 'cos' (because) show pronunciation which is very similar to sounds in general use in English. The main interest stems from the 'o' sounds in 'opeluss' (hopeless) and 'opun' (open) and 'over' which are all long and open sounds. The local pronunciation of the word 'only' has been known to cause confusion to strangers since the 'l' sound is often dropped, resulting in a word sounding something like 'oany'. Key words to consider here are 'trod' (past tense of tread) which emerges as 'trood', 'tooth' which sounds like 'twth' and 'comb' which is treated as though it is spelled 'coomb', Unlike English-speaking folk elsewhere, locals pronounce the word 'hour' as having two syllables so that in Wenglish, 'hour' rhymes with 'Gower' – *never* as 'ar' to rhyme with 'Gar'!

U It is surely this vowel sound which mostly distinguishes speakers of Wenglish since much of the unique flavour of local speech forms stems from this much-employed sound. The local pronunciation of this vowel seems to be the result of the Welsh word for God – 'Duw'. A reasonable approximation of its sound is offered by the word 'due', where full weight is afforded the 'u' sound. Perhaps this sentence will be found to have value here: 'Youer Heubutt (your Hubert), ower Rueth (our Ruth) and theyer Bruece (their Bruce) haven't got a clue how to get to Ruebyna (Rhiwbina). This pronunciation is echoed in 'fue' ('few'), 'yue' ('you'), 'nue' ('knew' and 'new'), 'grue' ('grew'), 'hue' ('hew', 'hue' and 'Hugh'), etc.

Notable exceptions are 'doos' for 'dues' (occasionally), 'ew' instead of 'yue' and although 'trues' ('trews') follows the local norm, only rarely does the word 'true' conform nowadays, since 'troo' seems to be more favoured. However, 'truth' is still 'trueth' in these parts. This vowel sound in turn affects the local sound for words like 'beautiful' (bue-tee-full), 'fruit' (fruete) 'cruise' (crueze') sluice' (sluese') and 'juice' ('juese') etc. Attention needs to be paid to words like 'furious' and 'curious' which are treated locally as having three distinct syllables – 'fue-ree-uss' and 'cue-ree-uss'.

The use – and abuse – of the aspirate in Wenglish continues to cause confusion to foreigners (both overseas and indigenous). The rules governing its use in local speech seem to be fairly simple: it is used whenever it is not needed, e.g., Haitch TV; Haitch P. Sauce; Haitch G. Wells, etc., and rarely used when it is required by the rules of standard English usage: 'ow the 'ell' , 'e's 'opeluss', 'e've got 'eaps of 'ealthy 'abits', etc.

The way in which the word 'local' is pronounced - 'lo-cull' - helps to demonstrate what happens to the final syllable of a number of words in Wenglish: 'hospitull' (hospital); 'genrull' (general); 'capitull' (capital); 'acceedunt' (accident); 'Cumarthun' (Carmarthen); 'scoundrull' (scoundrel) and 'reglur' (regular) are common examples. The words 'genrull' and 'reglur' show how, unlike standard English forms, words like these are afforded only two syllables in Wenglish speech forms.

How to 'Talk More Tidy'

The difficulties encountered in setting down in print many of the Wenglish words and phrases in common use are very real since some of the sound-blends employed are not covered by the conventions of standard English spelling. One solution would seem to be that offered by using a phonetic representation of sounds and words found in Wenglish. Such a presentation will, it is hoped, also offer a further guide to the way in which local people string together sounds and words.

This section, then, offers a selection of phonetically-represented phrases, sayings, and sentences, all of them readily heard in the everyday speech of people in the valleys communities. The 'decoding' of these merits attention since the exercise will, in turn, provide useful practice in getting one's tongue around local expressions, plus the best possible means of experiencing the rhythms and cadences of Wenglish speech in action. An added bonus for undertaking the exercise should be an understanding of the 'weighting' afforded to various syllables in these expressions, by trying them out at varying speeds when the basic 'decoding' has been done. Fluent Wenglish speakers will, I hope, carry out the task just for the fun of it.

To start you off, here are some easy examples with the correct version and, where required, the standard form, given immediately following them.

Wears ee to? (Where is he?) (Where's he to?)
Wine yue say en? (Why didn't you say, then?)
… oany iffee attoo . (… only if he had to.)
Doan kee pon! (Don't keep on!)
Wye zee sullong? (Why is he so long?)
Sup twim, eye spose. (It's up to him, I suppose)
War rue after isstime? (What are you after this time?)
… you gorrope! (… you've got a hope!)
Gissit year. (Give us it here.)
Years sumba there. (Here's some (by) there.)
Wodger won now en? (What do you want now, then?)
Jowonner nuther wunnervum or no? (Do you want another one of them or not?)

Longer examples: Answers on page 41 & 42

1. Eeel beer tie dee spell eye spect.
2. Cozzay wuz bard ay stay dome aft trawl.
3. Annie adder cheek ter say tin is folt tatall.
4. We been non twum bow tit issages bus sno yuse.
5. Wine ee say? Eee oany attoo mensh nitter me
6. Sauler cordin ter whorr eel say reelly.
7. Kee pewer rye out fur wunner vum.
8. Yule see now jest wattle appen twum.
9. Doanshee avver lorra potch with um?

10 Wear thee ell vee gone now jew spose?
11 Ee avven been slong time burree seddee wood.
12 Shop-pin downer pree sink? Eyem nor fust reelly!
13 Asser fack? Yue gorrw be joe-kin!
14 She din no witch waiter turn frim arfer time.
15 Nuff zee nuff eyeder say twum.
16 They woz orl air bar wunner vum.
17 Still lundy-sided ay yar bout go-in.
18 There stimes eye cood cry fie stopter think.
19 Gerrem cloze offer line, iss cummin nonto rain.
20 Doan kee pon lue? Airs nun frew iss time.
21 She car-reedit inner ram barg.
22 Ease zafter sum-thin ruthe aller time, ease days.
23 Wosser time by yue? Wens top tap?
24 Kep nye on thar, eye gorrw slip pout fra spell.
25 Giv zit year or yule coppit!
26 Vue adder tie-dee swill? Lemmee see youer rands.
27 Ease tryna fig-rout oo did it twim.
28 Pylesa vums scummin fay cun avver day off.
29 Lue be downer club lay-tron or no?
30 Eel lafto leave-vit go cozzease ger rin onner bit now.
31 Off-full wunnee iz friz pie-clutts.
32 Lenth fizz tung zall she ad innee yend!
33 Fue doan warchit yule gerra good damrin!
34 No shay ponnim round thee ouse-prop-ram fisted e is!
35 Fue doan nyesht an stop all at grizzlin, eyel give yue whor for!
36 Thairs times eyeder wun-drizit wur thit!
37 Appee ter see the backer vum sheel bee rye-tee nuff!
38 Slong en, see yue wafter - yue cum nower rousse or me up youers?
39 Weel lafto cum ter summer rangement lay tron, eye spect.
40 Smatter a fack, ease gon thool og iss time!
41 Loose goal yue? Thar smine, nor ewers!
42 Sheave gone down wassnames an then shease offter see Wotchermacall.
43 Eye vard bout tall eye cun take iss time!
44 Chopsee wun an fuller clecs zee was, but eye soon choke tim off!
45 Fie doan see twit stray toff, snow yuser tall.
46 Pay-shunt tee was, luvvim!
47 Pity yelp us iffee take sover, fass saul ee cun do bough tit!
48 Ope-luss ee is, ee yavven gorra clue!
49 Kee pewer self tie-dee fra spell till ay rive year.
50 Mar-reed? Nevvur! Livin tal-lee thay yar rye-tee-nuff!
51 Easer fraydeal lafto avvit dunner gen.
52 We roff frolly days nown a cuppler munce.
53 Boyn narf ee is – addus laffin fittobust.
54 Quiter willin she was innee yend twavvit done frer.
55 Wide zee kee ponner bout tit wennee nose ease inner wrong?

7

56 Attoo avver bitterva wiff ee did cozzee woz outer puff.
57 In ee yend it gosso bard they attoo avit seento.
58 Eye larvitagen fass or right
59 Fie din no diffrunt eyed dreckun ease nor all air arfer time.
60 Wylie woz airy addiz air cutz well.
61 Airs normer chelse year now like, izz air reelly?

Advanced examples for the really confident

1. Eave been gowin now on nun off, back an fore, frages, burrit avunt dunnim orl la much good die reckun.
2. Saul ee sed bout tit, burriffee did – tampin she woz an keep non thee ool time ee woz there.
3. We ravvin sum dee in forra pape-rin, then eel afto gerron wither mulsh nin.
4. Eave gorrit inniz zed thar ease a reeal cert frit, burree avven gor rope in nell zie see it.
5. Owzee offers ticks ease days now eave giv nup workin downer pit?
6. Eye gorr wadmit eyeder feel eaps better ease days, betran eye been sages eye spose.
7. Wen toffer dee pend ee did, like ziffee atto, ee carn elp imself wennee dwarv wun viz bouts!
8. Potchin boutee woz, steader do nit tie dee zee wor spose to, burris no yuse keep non twim!
9. Iffee doany lissun! Burreye mite zwell giv tuppser bard job frall eeder care bout it.
10. Ease adder lotter potch tryna gessum close tersute tim, burrees fick stup now.
11. Eave gorron fame us reely, eave gorra lorramen undrim mat twerk.
12. Orrite ten, avvit chewer roan way, burriff twoz upter me, eyed show um a thinger two, saul eye gorrw say.

A Visitors' Guide to Local Place Names.

Much difficulty is experienced by 'strangers' with regard to the way in which local place names (many of them truly magnificent!) are pronounced. It is by no means to be thought that the following constitute some sort of 'approved-list'; it is, rather, a guide for strangers on how local people *usually* say them.

The syllable which is in italics in each example shows where the stress ought to be placed when saying these names.

A	Abercanaid	- Aber-*can*-id
	Abercynon	- Aber-*kun*-non (*Never* Aber-sign-on!)
	Abersychan	- Aber-*suck*-un
	Abertridwr	- Aber-*trid*-er
	Argoed	- *Ar*-god

B	Bargoed	- *Bar*-god
	Beddau	- *Bather* (as in someone swimming)
	Bedlinog	- Bed-*lin*-og
	Bedwellty	- Bed-*wel*-tee
	Bedwas	- *Bed*-wuss
	Blackwood	- *Black*-ood
	Blaina	- *Blay*-nuh
	Brithdir	- *Brith*-duh (ditto)
	Brynmawr	- Brim-*moor*

C	Caerwent	- *Car*-went
	Caerleon	- *Cuh*-leen (*Cu*-leen)
	Caerffili/	
	Caerphilly	- Cuff-*illy*
	Caer-Rhacca	- *Cuh*-racker
	Caerau	- *Ky*-ruh
	Cilfynnydd	- Kill-*vun*-ith/Kill
	Cwmbrân	- Cum-*brân*
	Cymmer	- *Cum*mer
	Croesyceiliog	- Crossy-*kill*-og/Crossy-*keel*-og

D	Deri	- *Der*ry
	Dowlais	- *Dow*-luss
	Duffryn/Dyffryn	- *Duff*-rin

E	Efail Isaf	- Ev-*liss*-av – Ev-*lish*a
	Ebbw Vale	- Ebber-*Vale*

| **F** | Ffaldau | - *Fal*-der |
| | Fleur-de-Lys | - *Flo*wer |

G	Garn yr Erw	- Garn-er-*rue*
	Gelligaer	- Gelli-*gare*
	Gelli-wastad	- Gelli-*wast*-ud (Never 'Jelly-wasted!)
	Govilon	- Go-*vile*-un/Guh-*vile*-un
	Graigwen	- The Rock/Up the Rock
	Gwauncaegurwen	- GCG

H	Hafod-yr-Ynys	- Hav-od-*run*-iss
	Heol-y-Cyw	- Hale-er-*cue*
	Heol-y-Plwyf	- 'Ell-of-a-*pull* (!)
	Hirwaun	- *Er*-win

L	Llanbradach	- Lan-*brad*-uck
	Llandaf/Llandaff	- *Lan*-duff
	Llanedeyrn	- Lan-*edn*
	Llanfabon	- Lan-*vab*-on
	Llanfoist	- Lan-*foyst*
	Llanhilleth	- Lan-*hil*-uth
	Llanishen	- Lan-*ish*-un
	Llantarnam	- La-*tar*-num
	Llantwit-Fardre/	
	Llanilltyd-Fardref	- Lan-twit-*var*-druh
	Llanwonno	- Lan-*wun*-no

M	Machen	- *Mack*-un
	Maerdy	- *Mar*-dee
	Maesycoed	- Massie-*code*
	Maesycwmmer	- *Massi*e/Massie-*cumm*-er
	Margam	- *Mar*-gum
	Merthyr Tydfil	- *Merth*-er
	Morlais	- *Maw*-lice
	Mountain Ash	-Mount/Up the Mount.

| **N** | Nantyglo | - Nan-tee-*glo* |
| | Nantymoel | - Nant-tee-mole |

P Pencoed   - Pen-*code*
   Pencoedcae   - Pen-*koy*-ker
   Pengam   - *Peng*-gum
   Penpedairheol   - Pen-pedar-*real* (Or try 'Cascade')
   Penrhiwceiber   - *Ky*-ber/The Kyber
   Pentwyn   - Pen-*twin* (Cardiff pronunciation)
   Pentyrch   - Pen-*turk*
   Penyfai   - Pen-a-*vay*
   Pontardawe   - Pont-a-*daw*-wee
   Pontlottyn   - Pont-*lot*-in
   Pont Sion Norton   - Punch-in-*Nor*ton
   Pontsticill   - Pont-*stick*
   Pontypool   - Ponty/Pont-ee-pool
   Pontypridd   - Ponty/Pont-er-preeth/Pont-ee-preeth
   Porth   - Poth (to rhyme with the English 'both')
   Porthcawl   - Poth-*caul*
   Port Talbot   - Port-*tall*-but/Port-*tal*-bwt

R Radyr   - *Rad*-der
   Rhiwbina   - Rue-*by*-nuh
   Rhondda   - *Ron*-thuh
   Risca   - *Risk*-er
   Rhydlafar   - Rid-*lar*ver/Red-*lar*ver
   Rhydri   - *Rud*-ree
   Rydyfelin/Rhydfelen: - Rid-*vel*-un
   Rhymney/Rhumney   - *Rum*-nee

S Senghenydd   - Sin-*gen*-ith
   St. Mellons   - *Smell*-uns

T Talbot Green   - *Tal*-but Green/Tall-but Green
   Talywaun   - Tal-er-*wine*
   Tirphil   - Turf-*ill*
   Tiryberth   - Tirra-*berth* ('berth' to sound like 'birth')
   Tongwynlais   - Ton-*gwin*-luss
   Tonypandy   - Tonner-*pan*-dee (Never 'Tony' as in boy's name)
   Tonyrefail   - Ton-*rev*-ull
   Trecynon   - Tree-*kun*-nun
   Treharris   - Tree-*arris*/Charris
   Treherbert   - Tree-*er*-but
   Treoes   - Trose
   Treorci.Treorchy   - Tree-*or*-kee
   Troedyrhiw   - Troy-*droo*
   Trinant   - Try-nant

Y	Ynysboeth	- Unnis-er-*both*/The Both
	Ynysybwl	- Unnis-er-*bull*/The Bull
	Ystrad	- *Uss*-trad/*Uss*-trud
	Ystradmynach	- Uss-trad-*mun*-ack

This list is by no means exhaustive; many local examples of the mutation/mutilation of South Wales place-names will, I feel sure, be added by those who know their localities intimately.

Places a little further afield which are popular with local people include Ab-rav-un (Aberavon); Bah-ree-Eye-lun (Barry Island); Erry-ford (Hereford); Langlun Bay (Langland Bay); Lav-nock (Lavernock); Pem-brook (Pembroke); Puh-narth (Penarth); Po-tie-nun (Port Eynon); Ross-illy (Rhossili); Tem-bee (Tenby); The Gow-ur (*Never* 'Gar') (Gower); Tin-tun Nabbee (Tintern Abbey); Suther-down (Southerndown); Sim-munds Yot (Symonds Yat) and Cazwil Bay (Caswell Bay).

A Further Glossary of Wenglish Words, Phrases, and Expressions

The numerous suggestions for words and expressions for another Wenglish glossary sent by many people who have read *Talk Tidy* are gratefully and warmly acknowledged.

I am particularly grateful to those who took the trouble to compile lists of words and phrases which were in common use during the significant period when there was, for a majority of local people, a 'linguistic watershed' between the use of Welsh and the use of imported English words and expressions. This process inevitably led to the situation where there was a 'cut-off point' in the use of Welsh in many valley families. It was common in the large families which were usual in those days for the first two, three or four (and often, more) children to be brought up to speak Welsh on the hearth and for the subsequent offspring to be raised to speak only English.

One result of this social upheaval was the valley community phenomenon, viz. the child who was spoken to in Welsh by his older relatives and who replied always in English. It also produced countless people, paricularly in my generation, who understand Welsh but cannot themselves speak it.

Inevitably, the switch over to the widespread use of English, whether gradual or abrupt in pace, produced many problems for older people who were compelled to engage in the often painful process of trying to use the difficult and complicated language called English, rather than their natural mode of expression - Welsh. This resulted in the accounts – real or apocryphal – given by many of my contemporaries of grandparents and other older relatives who spoke of someone who 'was living two doors lower up' or who rounded off statements with expressions like '… me too, neither, isn't it?'

So-called true accounts of the speech of older family members probably stem from youthful efforts at parodying the quaint speech which they often heard. The validity of such quoted utterances as '… if I had respected you, I would have repaired for you …' is always questionable after so prolonged a lapse of time, but I have to confess to a great liking for the following story: The aged relative was having great problems in her attempts to speak English and matters were brought to a head by the arrival of twins in the family. There came the day when the two lively boys, now aged about four were visiting the old lady. She encountered one of them in the garden and said, "Tell me now, 'machgen i (my boy) – is it yue or yuer brother?"

There can be no doubt, though, that one reason why Wenglish retains the rhythms, cadences, and inflections of Welsh speech is because 'new' imported words were taken on board in local speech only when they had been 'treated' in order to make them sound like Welsh words.

Three much-used local words seem to me to typify this definitive process of word-assimilation: 'ours', 'yours' and 'theirs'. Elsewhere in the United Kingdom where I have lived for significant periods, I noted that each of these words is monosyllabic and their respective pronunciations sound to me, at least, like 'ares', yores' and 'theres'/'thairs'. In Wenglish, each of these key words has two definite syllables and they are sounded as 'ouers/owurs', 'yue-ers'/'yew-urs' and 'thayers/thayurs' with Welsh-sounding inflection added for good measure to produce sounds which enable speakers of Wenglish to be readily identified in 'foreign parts'.

Like the glossary offered in *Talk Tidy* this one undoubtedly includes words, phrases, and expressions which are found also in standard English utterances. However, it is because they have undergone the 'Wenglishisation process' to make them sound as if they were derived from Welsh roots, that they are included.

The manner in which words are employed gives an especial social connotation to local language since it affords positive clues to the people who speak thus – their values, their prejudices and preferences, and their outlook on life in general. A useful example of this is provided by the local expression 'a bit o …', and I am truly grateful for his comments to a former colleague of my days in North Wales who is now a very senior educationalist there. A native of the Amman Valley, he lived for some years in Port Talbot. He offers an escalating series of descriptions used in Port Talbot when the Abbey Steel Works (known locally as 'The Klondyke') opened. An ordinary process worker was known simply as being 'down the Abbey'. A foreman would be known as 'a bit of a boss down the Abbey', whilst a manager would invariably be known as a 'big noise down the Abbey'.

He goes on to say, 'I personally love the expression "a bit of a boss" because it encapsulates all the scepticism/populism/rebelliousness/refusal to take anyone/anything *too* seriously that to me is the essence of South Wales.

A number of correspondents took me – gently, firmly (but rightly) – to task for not showing the full extent of local usage afforded to certain words. A good example of this is the word 'gambo'; I have tried my 'level best' to put this right this time.

I am now firmly convinced that it is impossible for one person to compile a definitive and exhaustive glossary of Wenglish words, phrases, and sayings. So many people continue to send, give, and suggest so many examples of words at work in Wenglish, that I am forced to the conclusion that there are many words being used in local communities which are 'local' in the narrowest sense of the word – and some which are peculiar to certain local *families* only.

This second attempt at a glossary is offered, therefore, in the hope that it will produce the same effect as the first, i.e. that of ensuring that many people will read it and supplement it either with words and sayings which and their families use, or with those which they recall from days past. The most desirable end-result is, in my opinion, that pride in our distinctive and unique local lingo will be engendered and deepened by all those who share this common heritage.

Glossary

A

A king to: Very much better than, as in, 'Oh 'e's 'eaps better – 'e's a king to what 'e was lass week!"

About: Wenglish for 'out and about', 'She've been bard, but she's about agen now ...'

(H)ad it (h)ard: Found things very difficult; 'She've 'ad it 'ard this years, pooer dab, with all them mouths to feed!'

Afraid to open my mouth: Wary of comment; 'I'm afraid to open my mouth, gone with 'im! Jump right down my throat, 'e do!"

Agen/Again: (1) Different, as 'That's another pair agen she've got'.
           (2) Also; 'You ought to put that by there again.'

All along: All the time, as in, '... pretendin 'e didn't twig – 'e knew all along!'

All came back: Recalled all the details; 'When I told 'im off, it all came back to 'im what 'e'd promised.'

All up with: 'The end of the line', as in, 'I reckon it's all up with him now pooer dab.'

Always on: Always harping on; "Give it a rest will yue? – youer always on about something or other all the time!'

Always on the road: Wenglish for someone who is constantly out and about.

'am been well: Hasn't or haven't been well; 'I/She am been well this ages.'

And there was me thinkin': And there was I supposing; 'They 'aven't got two 'apenies to rub together and there was me thinkin' they was rollin' in it.'

Answer the door: See who is at the door.

Anyhow: Anyway/In any case, as in, 'I was goin' to the party anyhow!'

Appro (on): Having goods on approval.

Arm/Back/Knee/Leg went: A favoured local xpression to show that some part of the anatomy has 'given-out' or developed a weakness; 'No gul, I couldn't go to chapel last week – my leg went!'

Ashamed: As in standard English, but a much-favoured local expression; 'I'd have been ashamed for anyone to see the state it was in.'

Atto laugh: Wenglish for 'had to laugh.'

At-ue-a/Atwa: Wenglish for 'that you are!' 'You're a cheeky devil, atwa!'

Awa: Old Wenglish for 'uncle' – the masculine of 'bopa'

Awful: Awfully, as in, 'He's awful bard today.'

Awful for: Over fond or over-dependent; 'That kid of theyers is awful for 'is mother.'

Aye: An emphatic term, as in, 'There was 'eaps there aye!"

B

Babi lol/Babi loshin: A real baby, an over-indulged child. Surviving Welsh terms.

Bad job: A hopeless case; 'I atto give it up as a bad job in the end.'

Bald-headed: (1) Going at a job over-vigorously, as in, 'e went at the gardnin' (gardening) real bald-'eaded!'
           (2) Responding over-emphatically in an argument; 'When I told 'im that, 'e went for me bald-'eaded!'

Banjo: A very local word (Aberdare – and elsewhere?) for a loaf of bread, more commonly called a 'batch'.

Bard-minded: Used to describe someone who always thinks the worst of others.

Bare-faced liar: A much-used expression for teller of 'whoppers'.

Bare week/fortnight etc: A week/fortnight etc. and no more.

Be for your life: Take extreme care; 'When them kids are here I gorrw be for my life with 'em – into everything, they are!'

Beauty of it: The distinct advantage; '… and the beauty of it is, it washes like a rag …'

Bein/Being I was: Since I was already, as in, 'Bein' as I was goin' there, I thought I'd pop in to see them.'

Bished: Tired out

Bit of: (1) A popular expression used thus: 'I'm off to have my bit of dinner, now' and 'I managed to get a bit of fish for my dinner'.

(2) It is also used to show minimal competence, as in, 'Oh yes, 'e cun play a bit on the piano.'

Bit pushed: A little short of, as in, 'I can't stop now, I'm a bit pushed for time' or 'I can't get it now, I'm a bit pushed for money.'

Blaggud: The favoured Wenglish pronunciation of 'blackguard'

Blas halen: A surviving Welsh expression meaning 'savoury'; I'm nothing for old sweet stuff, gone, give me something blas halen every time!'

Bonc: A surviving Welsh expression for a blow. A 'bonclust' is to have one's ear 'boxed' ('clust' – Welsh for ear).

Boo nor Bah: Nothing at all, as in 'She've got 'im right there! – 'e don't say boo nor bah to nothin'!'

Born in a field: An expression used to someone who constantly leaves doors open – 'Were you born in a field or somethin'?'

Boy narf/Boy-and-a-half: Something of a character, as in 'Boy narf 'e is, for shuer – never know what 'e'll come out with next!'

Brat: A word from Welsh, meaning an apron; rarely heard nowadays.

Brem butter: Wenglish for bread and butter.

Brocclo: The favoured local pronunciation for 'broccoli'.

Bundle of nerves: Much-used locally to describe a very nervous person.

Buried his wife/buried he husband: A common local expression to show that someone has been bereaved; 'She buried her husband last month.' Strangers have been known to enquire whether the bereaved spouse actually carried out the interment!

Buzz off: A much-used expression for 'clear off!'

By rights: According to the laws of justice; 'She should have had that after her mother, by rights!'

By the looks of it: From all appearances, as in, ' 'E've cleared off an' 'e's not comin' back, by the looks of it!'

C

Cabolach: A rarely-used word nowadays, it means 'in a mess' or 'mixed up'

Caib: A Welsh word for a useful, double-sided tool for digging and hoe-ing (cf.

Pickaxe/mattock).

Calling you everything: Saying all manner of unpleasant things about you; 'Calling you everything, she was, when you didn't turn up!'

Cam-Bryan: The favoured pronunciation, in some local areas, for 'Cambrian'.

Came up trumps: Fulfilled all expectations – and more! Quiet sort of bloke he seemed, but when he had to make that speech, he came up real trumps!'

Caper; A trick or a ploy, as in, 'She caught me out once, but she won't get away with that caper again.'

Carn afford/Can't afford: Cannot take the risk, as in, 'She've been ill this ages so she carn afford to catch another cold on top of it.'

Carn/Can't put up with: Cannot stand or bear; 'I'm tellin' you straight, I carn put up with all this quarrellin' round here!'

Carying on: (1) Keeping on about something; 'All this carrying on! It's high time you forgot it now.'

(2) Having an illicit relationship, as in, '… only been married a spell an 'e's carryin on with somebody at work.'

Cera!: Still heard occasionally, this Welsh word means 'Get on with you' (literally, it means 'go').

Chapel lossin/loshin: A long-lasting sweet (usually of the mint-humbug variety), so-called because it was often popped into the mouth at the beginning of the sermon.

Cheap tack: Something regarded as being inferior in quality.

Chopped: Favoured local pronunciation for 'chapped'.

Chwps/Choops: To an extreme state; '… last night again; 'e drunk 'imself chwps.' Or 'In a state, she was – cried herself chwps.'

Clip: A blow, as in, 'A clip 'side the yearole/earhole is what you're askin' for.' The word 'flip' was sometimes used to express something similar.

Click: Wenglish for 'clique'. People can be described as 'clicky'.

Clicks: A local expression for 'head-lice'. Also called 'chicks' and 'chickeroos'.

Clicked: Been successful, as 'Goin' steady they are – 'e seems to 'ave clicked there this time …'

Clod: Although I do not recall hearing or using this word, I am assured that it was once widely used locally thus: 'Picked a hool lot a blackberries for 'em, I did – an' they din even give me a clod!' I am further assured that 'clod' is an old name for a penny.

Clonc: A good old chat/gossip with a neighbour. 'Clonc' is the Welsh word for 'gossip'.

Clwb claddu: Savings for burial purposes. The expression, which is Welsh, means, literally, 'burial club'.

Cochyn/Cwchyn: A Welsh expression for a red-headed person.

Colly: The favoured local word for 'cauliflower'.

Come out with: Say, as in 'A real case 'e is! The things 'e do come out with!'

Come over 'im/'er: Affected him/her strangely, as in, 'it's like as if something do come over 'im now an' agen!'

Coming (on) to rain/snow: Starting to rain/snow

Come to go: Take one's departure, as in the old Wenglish expression, 'It's time for us to come to go.'

Conk: A local expression, not heard as often currently, for 'nose'. Also used for 'head'.

Consid(e)rin(g): When all is considered; 'A real cop (bargain) it was, considrin'!'

Convalassunt: A one-time favoured pronunciation of 'convalescent'.

Costiff; An old word which was once used in these parts for 'constipated'. 'Costive' is an old English word.

Costin(g) them somethin(g): Very expensive; 'It's costin' them somethin' to keep that horse, I cun tell you.'

Couldn't get over it: Couldn't really believe it; 'They couldn't get over it when they had a house to themselves at last.'

Could tell by her: Could tell by looking at her; 'All quiet she was, but you could *tell* by her she was upset, alright!'

Cozzee/Cozzay: Wenglish for 'because he' and 'because they'.

Crackin' laughin/Cracking laughing: Laughing very heartily.

Cree: Immunity in a children's game.

Cribbin(g): In addition to meaning 'cheating by copying' as in standard English, this has a Wenglish meaning – 'complaining'.

Cried like the rain: Cried a very great deal.

Crimped up: Slumped, as in, 'Gone to look bard, she 'ave – she do walk about all crimped up.'

Cronjy/Crogie: A very close, short haircut.

Cryin(g) blue murder: Making a very great 'palaver' when upset.

Crying out for more: Making earnest requests for, as in, 'They can't keep up with it in the shops – they're all crying out for more!'

Cue-cummer: Wenglish for 'cucumber'.

Curling box (1) This was a wide, large scoop for carrying coal when a 'load of coal' had been delivered. The small coal was then 'riddled' and the pieces which were too large to go through the mesh (quite small pieces) were called 'curlings'.
(2) When the ashes were 'riddled', the pieces too large to pass through were known as 'cols'.

Cwrdd clecs: Sadly not heard much nowadays, this Welsh expression is a sardonic description of a ladies' meeting. Literally, it means a meeting where clecs (gossip, tittle-tattle) are exchanged.

D

Dal (not much): The Welsh verb 'dal' means a number of things, amongst them 'hold', 'catch' or 'continue'. 'There's not much dal on this material.'

Deal: To give custom to, as in, 'I don't deal in that shop any more – there's not much shape to them now.'

Deceiving: Misleading; 'There's deceiving for you – looks like it holds plenty, but you can only get half a pint in it.'

Diws annwyl/Deuce ynnwl: A fairl mild local expletive derived from 'Duw annwyl' meaning 'Dear God'.

Dibs/Dib up: When you 'dib up' you pay your 'dibs', i.e. you pay your contributions or debts.

Dicky show your light: A children's game of days gone by, involving a piece of candle in a string-held tin in a variation of 'hide-and-seek', played on dark evenings.

Didn't mind a bit: Didn't care at all.

Dimp: A word recalled from childhood meaning 'a bit "twp" or "simple" '

Din 'ave (didn't have) the decency: Didn't show common courtesy; 'She din 'ave the decency to tell me, an' she knew I'd been after one this ages.'

Dim ots: No odds; it doesn't matter; it makes no difference. Not heard as often as it once was; 'Well, dim ots, if they haven't got any, I can manage fine.'

Dinnit? Wenglish for 'didn't it?'

Diprish: Untidy, slovenly. (Old Wenglish).

Diraen/Dee rane: A Welsh expression meaning 'lacking in sparkle' – having no 'grain' (graen) on it.

Doan wonnoo: Wenglish for 'I don't want to.'

Do anything with him/her: An expression showing pleasing amenability.

Doesn't rise to: Is not sufficient for; 'Thass not mine – my pay don't rise to one like that …'

Doing a Martha and Mary: Referring to two people (as in the Bible story) – one doing all the work whilst the other takes it easy.

Done a bunk: Has cleared off; 'They've done a bunk – you'll never see youer money now!'

Donkey-work: The difficult/unpleasant parts of a task, as in, 'Oh, she did all the paperin(g) but I was the muggins who had to do all the donkey-work getting(g) it all prepared!'

Don't know how to take him/her: Don't know how to 'read' him/her; 'He comes out with some funny expressions – I don't know how to take him half the time.'

Don't last five minutes: Is very soon gone; 'Destructive's not the word for 'im! You buy 'im somethin' to play with an' it don't last five minutes with 'im.!'

Don't talk!: You haven't heard the half of it! 'Don't talk – I got one of those, too – and mine's much worse than yours …'

Don't look!: This has always seemed to me, at least, a most contradictory expression since it invites the opposite outcome to that stated; 'Don't look at the state of this place – I haven't had time to get started on the work yet!!'

Door went: 'The door went' means that someone had knocked the door or had rung the door bell.

Doss: A nap or brief spell of sleep; 'I told her to lie down and have a little doss for a spell.'

Drag: A difficult journey, as in, 'It's a long old drag to where they've gone to live now.'

Drama: A one-time favoured word for a play of any type.

Drash/trash: A word used in parts of Gwent (and elsewhere?) for work on hedges. 'Trash is an old English word for hedge-cuttings or broken twigs and drash would seem to be a mutation of this word.

Drovers: Old Wenglish word for 'drawers'.

Dry: Having a droll sense of humour. Someone having this is sometimes said to be 'as dry as a chip'.

Dubs: The lavatories, the WCs especially in school – in my childhood, at least. 'Dub' is an abbreviation of WC.

Dwnshee/Doanshee?: Wenglish for 'doesn't she?' 'Dwnshee keep it nice?'

Dwy'wech am swllt: Literally the Welsh expression means 'Two sixpences for a shilling'. It was used to mean feeling less than well. 'I don't feel right at all – I'm like dwy'wech am swllt today.'

E

Eapsa: Wenglish for 'heaps of'.

Ee-ya-boy! An often heard local form of call to a dog.

Eli for every clwy: A splendid example of the co-existence of Welsh and English in local speech. It is a part-translation of 'eli i bob clwyf' – 'an ointment for every sore'. It was used to describe someone who always had an excuse to cover all sorts of eventualities; 'It's no use trying to get sense from him about what happened – he's got an eli for every clwy, that one!'

Enjoy: The non-reflexive use of this verb was heard frequently in childhood days when an oft-posed question from older relatives was, 'Did you enjoy?'

End of the quarter: In homes where Welsh was spoken, this was known as 'pen-cwarter' or 'pen cwarter siop'. In the days when the Co-op. was probably the leading, non-independent local store, the end of the quarter was a significant event since it was the time when it was essential to 'clear the Co-op book' and get one's accounts in order. This recalls those far-off days when (for our family, at least) the 'dividend' made all the difference between 'paying your way' and failing to do so.

Enough to put years on you: Although I seem not to hear, 'It's enough to put years on you!' as often as I used to, this plaintive cry is still a feature of local speech.

Every ... like the clock!: With unfailing regularity, as in, ' 'E' do never miss – 'ere every Wednesday like the clock, 'e is!'

Eyes everywhere: Inquisitive, prying, as in, 'You'll have to keep that cwtched when she comes – she's got eyes everywhere, that one!'

Eyes in the back of my head: Although this is not peculiar to Wenglish, it is included because in a context of Wenglish it does have a distinctive local flavour, viz. 'You gorrw 'ave eyes in the back of youer 'ead!'

F

Fagged out: (This was listed in 'Talk Tidy' but I omitted to explain its origin.) Very tired, and almost surely a derivation of the Welsh word 'diffygio' which means 'to be tired'.

Fancy man/woman: The person with whom an illicit affair is going on; 'She've only been married less than a twelmunth an' she've got a fancy man in the place she works.'

Fell: An old Wenglish word to mean 'dropped' as in, 'I fell my sweet in the gutter.'

Fetched him one: Gave him one, as in, 'A mouthful was all I had, so I fetched him one across his chops!' A variation of this is seen in, 'I gave him a fetcher!'

Figure it out: It is the way in which this is usually said which ensures its inclusion here; 'I told 'im 'e'd affto figrit out frim self.'

Fire half way up the chimney: This recalls vividly the type of fire often seen in colliers' homes and still describes a very good fire today.

First goin(g) off: This, together with 'last goin(g) off', shows a variation of 'first go off' and 'last go off 'which are Wenglish for 'first thing' and 'last thing'.

Fit to bust: In an extreme fashion, as in, 'By the time they'd finished he was laughing/shouting fit to bust.' Also thus, 'I've eaten fit to bust!'

Fixed (how are you?): How are you placed? As in, 'How are you fixed for getting back an' fore to see him in hospital?'

Flannen: The way in which the word 'flannel' was always pronounced when I was young (and sometimes today). The Welsh word for 'flannel' is 'gwlanen'.

Flat shot: An anti-climax, or something which fails to live up to expectations. This expression, most frequently encountered in Gwent, seems to refer to a 'shot', (placed by the 'shot-firer' in the colliery) which fails to go off.

Flea-bite: A very small amount; 'I wanted a lot, not a flea-bite like this.'

Flush/flushed: Having plenty of money, as in, 'You better ask 'im for it now, while 'e's flush.'

Fly: Crafty; a 'fly' person is one who is always quick to seek his own advantage. 'You better watch out with 'im – a real fly one 'e is!'

For everlastin(g): Constantly, as in, 'That kid of theyers is one for everlastin' back and fore, back and fore, after somethin' or other all the time.'

For every day: For wearing on days other than Sundays, as in, 'No gul, I don't keep it for Sundays – it's for every day, now!'

For you!: Direct translation from the Welsh has produced sayings like 'There's posh for you!' or 'There's luck for you!'

Fork out: Pay up; 'I can't keep up with that boy and his shoes – I've just had to fork out twenty pounds for another pair for him!'

Forrid: Wenglish for 'forehead'.

Fry: Liver to Wenglish folk; '… and don't forget to ask the butcher for some pig's fry.'

Full-force: (1) Using all one's strength, as in, 'The door was stuck so he had to push full-force to get it open.'

(2) 'With no holds barred', '… I'd had enough and I had to have it out with her so I let her have it full-force!'

Full of himself: Showing a sense of his own importance; 'chesty'. (Arrogant people are often described thus.)

Fuss and feathers: Extracting the last bit of the possibilities of a situation and making a great 'to do' about it; 'Look at 'er – she's all fuss and feathers about goin' to that dance!'

G

Gavul/Gafael: Substance, quality, as in, 'There's not much gavul on these

22

sheets/pillow-slips' etc. One of the meanings of the Welsh word 'gafael' is 'substance'.

Gambo: Although this (a farm cart) was included in the *Talk Tidy* glossary, I have rightly been taken to task for not including its use as the word for a home-made wooden cart, usually with old pram wheels. 'Gambo' was the word applied, also to bicycles and even cars in a state of some disrepair.

Get about: Go out and about freely; 'She've been bothered with her legs frages, so she can't get about like she used to.'

Get the food goin(g): Begin to cook the meal, as in, 'They'll be 'ere now jest, so I better get theyer food goin' '

Give: Forecast, as in, 'On the wyluss (wireless) they give rain today in the weather.'

Give in: Confess, admit, as in, 'Give in, will you? We all know it was you that did it.'

Give what for!: An unspecified threat, as in, 'If you don't shape you(r)self, I'll give you what for in a minute!'

Glad of that: Pleased to have it; 'Beter take youer mac – you'll be glad of that if it comes to rain.'

Goin(g): Making for; 'Don't often see you on the train – Ponty. you goin(g) is it?

Gone: (1) Reached a point; 'She's real 'alf-soaked gone, lately!'
(2) More than one person has told me, in recent months, 'These books of yours – they're all over the world gone!'

Gone clean out of his/her head: Completely forgotten, as in, 'Gone clean out of 'is 'ead, it 'ad, about givin' me 'and with this!'

Gone lost: Favoured Wenglish term for 'lost'; 'I've been out this ages – my husband will think I've gone lost!'

Gone off: (1) Departed; 'They've gone off on another outing again.'
(2) Unfit for eating; 'Them pears are gone off!'
(3) Lost interest in; 'I don't eat them anymore – I'm gone right off them now.'

Good scholar: Those showing academic promise at school were always called 'good scholars'.

Go: Energy, enthusiasm, as in, 'There's no go in me at all these days.'

Got him/her: When he/she is being sociable, as in, 'There's no depends on him whether he'll speak to you or not – you never know when you've got him …'

Got on: Prospered; 'E've got on well – 'e's a reeal big noise.'

Governess/Guvness: The name always given to infant school head-teachers in days gone by.

Grand!: At a rapid rate; 'She's going through (using up) that money grand!' This of course, shows disapproval.

Groping: Tickling trout/or other fish. (I am assured that this is what this word implied in areas north of Bridgend!)

Gul: Girl, as in, 'You know gul, he's the one I saw in the Bracchi's now jest.'

Guts: A greedy one, as in, 'Real guts that one is – there's no filling 'im to be had!'

H

Had a gutsful: Had more than enough; this remark is obviously slightly less 'up-market' than a 'bellyful'.

Hair off: In a temper: 'He had his hair off proper when he heard about them carrying on like that!' The opposite expression is 'keep youer 'air on!'

Half his time/'alf 'is time: Much of the time; ' 'ow cun 'e say 'e works reg'lar – 'alf 'is time 'e's never there!'

Half-tidy: In certain (eastern) areas where Wenglish is spoken, this expression shows approval. I am told that in such areas, and in Cardiff, the ultimate is 'three-parts-half-tidy!'

Hammer/'Ammer (that's the): Another expression showing approval; 'Thass thee 'ammer!' (that's the 'ammer).

Hanes: Tale or report, as in, 'When I got 'er to myself, she told me the hool (whole) hanes'. 'Hanes is the Welsh word for the same context.

Had his hands full: Was fully occupied; 'He had his hands full with the two kids to see to while his wife was away.'

Hard lines: Unfortunate; 'It's real 'ard lines on 'er, pooer dab – she 'aven't done nothin' to deserve that!'

Havin(g) me on: Pulling my leg, as in, 'Cera! (Go on!) You're 'avin' me on, right enough!!'

Hawk: Carry. It has a slightly different meaning locally from the standard English meaning; 'After buying it all, you've got to hawk it all back with you.'

(H)eart an' soul: *Very* enthusiastic. 'e's 'eart an' soul in the Legion – there evry whip-stitch, 'e is!!'

Heavily-frueted/'eavily-frueted: A cake blessed with much fruit.

Hobbles: Illicit work, 'Supposed to be on the dole 'e is, but he's doin' plenty of 'obbles.'

Hollo: Thoroughly; 'Next time, we'll beat 'em 'ollo!'

Hool/'ool: Wenglish for 'whole'.

Houseful staying: Lots of visitors.

Hwylus: This Welsh word is sometimes used in reply to the query as to how one is feeling – 'Not very hwylus this morning' means the person is not feeling very well.

I

Iffeedid!: Wenglish for 'If he did!' 'Iffeedid! I soon squared 'im!'

I'm frightened of: I'm concerned about, as in, 'I got to wear this hat 'cos I'm frightened of my 'ead!'

In a huff: In great dudgeon, as in, 'When I had it out with her about the clecs she's been carrying, off she went in a huff!'

In by there: The sort of neighbourly remark often heard – 'How's youer mother/father/wife/etc. in by there today?'

In case: In case it is needed; 'I know it doesn't look like rain but take your mac, in case!'

In his oils: Listed and explained in the *Talk Tidy* glossary but I omitted to show its Welsh origin for 'in his element'. The original Welsh expression is 'Yn ei hwyliau' which, via mutations like 'in his hwyls' became finally, 'in his oils'.

Inshee?: Wenglish for 'isn't she!'

In the same sack: In the same category; 'Bad as one another they are – put 'em in the same sack, you could!'

J

Jasper/Rasper: A fine one; 'That's a real jasper/rasper you got there!'

Jibog: Old Wenglish for 'a funny face'

Jingalers: Old Wenglish meaning a hanging decoration on an ornament, or flashing jewellery.

Jinny fetw: The full name for 'jinny' or 'jenny' (punishment cane). 'Bedw' (often pronounced betw/fetw) is Welsh for a birch tree.

Joe Blunt: A person, of either sex, well-known for plain-speaking.

Jonic/Jonick: Genuine, honest, as in, 'you had me on last time, is it jonic this time?" (I am uncertain of the spelling, never having seen this word in print.)

Just/jest: (1) In the immediate past, as in, 'He've just/jest come, now!'

(2) Nearly; 'Pooer dab, 'E've been bard – 'e just/jest died!'

Just had enough: A common expression showing that someone has had about as much as he/she can take; 'Im telling you straight – I've just had enough of this caper.'

Just the same: Unspoilt by success, as in, 'I haven't seen her this years – got on well, she have, but she's just the same, no old swank with her!'

K

Keepin(g): Faring, as in, 'Eye-ya kid. 'ow you keepin these days?

Keep youer eye out: Maintain a sharp look out; 'They'll be here soon, so keep youer eye out frum! (for them).'

K'nye arv?: A local form of 'Can I have?'

Knock about with: Keep company with, as in, 'e's more steady now, but 'e used to knock about with a funny lot.'

Know 'im/'er of old: Recall what he/she is capable of from days long gone by; 'Ask 'im to do it for us? – Never!! I know 'im of old – potch it, 'e will!'

Knowin(g): Precocious; advanced; 'It's hard to believe that kid of theyers is only that age – he's very knowin(g)!' Another word often used in this context is 'forward'.

Know the ins and outs: To discover all there is to know, as, 'That kid of next-door's wants to know the ins and outs of a cat's behind!'

L

Landed back: Arrived home, as in, 'Trust us to be on the bus that broke down – half-past two it was when we landed back here!'

Lay my hand on: Find; 'I've searched everywhere for it but I can't seem to lay my hand on it anywhere!'

25

Lay off: Desist, give up, as in, 'Lay off will yue (you) – nuffsee-nuff!' (enough's enough).

Learn sense: Learn to do better; 'There's times I do wonder will 'e ever learn sense at all?!'

Leave alone: Let alone, as in, 'There's enough to do with the washing, leave alone the cooking …'

Leave it there: Let it be; 'Leave it there, will you? – I've had enough of you two arguing all the time.'

Leg under him: Support, as in, 'Not a leg under 'im there was, when 'e left that pub!'

Lemme: Wenglish for 'Let me.'

Length of one's tongue: A good telling-off; 'Got the length of 'er tongue 'e did – asking for it 'e was!'

Lick and a spit: A hurried and inadequate wash (in the bosh, of course!) This was something called 'a quick lick and a promise', or 'a cat's lick and a promise,'

Like a hopping jinny: Constantly on the move to the irritation of others; 'Sit still carn yue? (can't you?) you're like a hopping jinny all over the shop!'

Like as if: As if, as in, 'I don't know what gets into him, it's like as if he can't help himself half the time!'

Like, see!: Very much used in local speech; 'Goin' along, mindin' 'is own business 'e was when it 'appened, like see!'

Like a dog's dinner: A variation of 'dressed up to the nines', as in, 'I saw 'er goin off – all done up like a dog's dinner, she was!'

Like a pin in paper: *Very* clean and 'up-together;' 'Like a pin in paper, she is – you could eat off the floor with her!!'

Like a ton of bricks: Very heavily, as in, 'I only made one mistake but they were down on me like a ton of bricks!'

Like canal barges: Too large; 'These shoes I got are like canal barges on me!'

Line-ful: A good deal of washing on the clothes line; 'A line-ful I had out when it started to rain nasty!'

Llaw bwt: Welsh and Wenglish for 'left-handed', sometimes suggesting awkwardness.

Long-winded: Taking a long time over something, as in, 'He promised faithful to have it finished by now, but he's very long-winded about it!'

Look! See, as in, 'If you haven't got it on you now, I'll have it agen (again – later on) look!

Looking everywhere: Searching in every possible place, as in, 'I'm real danted (daunted) now, I been looking everywhere for them gloves of mine but I can't lay my hands on them, anywhere!'

Loosed (go): This expression refers to a child releasing his mother's hand and attempting to walk, as in, ' 'Ave 'e loosed go yet?'

M

Made out he/she was: Pretended that he/she was; '… made out 'e din (didn't) know nothin(g) about it – an' I was there when they asked 'im!'

Mad'nin': Maddening, infuriating, as in, 'Mad'nin' it is, there's somethin' or other all the time with 'er!'

Make two of: Very much larger than, as in, 'A real boilin(g) piece, she is – make two of *'im,* she would!'

Makin(g) for: Intending to go to; 'Where you makin(g) for this time, then?'

May have; Might have; 'e may 'ave been there, but I'm not sure a bit!'

Might as well talk to the wall: An exercise in sheer futility, as in, 'Might as well talk to the wall as talk to 'im – 'e don't take a blind bit a notice of me!'

Milgi: Welsh for greyhound, still occasionally heard locally.

Missed a chalk: Missed an opportunity; '... should have been ready you know – missed a chalk there, you did!'

Mootch: Sometimes used as an alternative to 'mitch' (play truant).

More fuss than the worth of it: Never worth all the bother; 'By the time I do get both of 'em ready, I do think it's more fuss than the worth of it, sometimes.'

Most likely: With a fair degree of certainty, as in, 'He's not here – you'll most likely find him down the park.'

Muckle-dee-dun: Strange, as in, 'I don't know, but it's been a muckle-dee-dun sort of day, really.'

Mun: Used in speaking to a male; 'Buck youer ideas up, mun!' or 'Well, aye, mun – thass (that's) where 'e've gone!'

Mynew: Wenglish for 'mind you'.

N

Neely/Nearly had a fit: Occasioning very great impact; 'When 'e told me how much it was, I neely 'ad a fit!'

Never all there: Regularly showing strange behaviour, as in, 'Don't never pay any attention to 'im – 'e's never all there!'

Never year (hear) the end of it: The 'palaver' about it continues; 'Don't touch that! If you break it, you'll never hear the end of it from your father!'

Newsy Landers: How many Wenglish folk talk of New Zealanders.

Niff: Strange smell, as in, 'Jew, there's a funny niff in by here!'

No age: Still far from old; '...buried 'im last week? – pooer dab – no age, was 'e?

No end: Extremely; Continually; 'It do worry me no end, the way they do carry on!'

No go at all: Lacking energy and enthusiasm, as in, '... 'alf-soaked! – there's no go in 'er at all!'

No knowin(g): No way of knowing, as in, 'Nothin(g)'s too 'ot or too 'eavy for that one – there's no knowin(g) what 'e'll be up to next!'

No looks on: Lost liking for; 'Since they cleaned it for me, I've got no looks on it at all!'

Nor friends/Norra frens/Not friends: No longer having anything to do with; 'I'm nor frens to 'er – she've 'ad it now!'

Nor willin(g)/Norra willin(g): Not willing; 'It's no use, she's norra willin(g) for us to 'ave it!'

Nor willin(g) a bit: Definitely not willing.

Nosso bard: Not so bad.

Not all there: See 'never all there'.

Not fussed: Not very keen, as in, 'They're after me all the time to go, but I'm not fussed, reelly (really).'

Not much upstairs: Lacking intelligence; 'E do do 'is best, I s'pose (suppose), but 'e 'aven't got much upstairs.'

Not sorry a bit: Lacking contrition, as in, 'He's done it and he's been threatening to do it for ages – and he's not sorry a bit!'

Now, after: In a short space of time, as in, 'If you'll only be a bit patient, I'll let you have them now, after!'

***Now* iss gone, look!/Now it's gone, look!:** Only now has it gone; 'That train was supposed to go at nine – but only *now* iss gone!'

Not in it!: Not to be described like that; 'Idle's not in it – be in bed all day she would, if you let her!'

O

'O' called after name: Locally, the letter 'o' is added when calling to a friend; as in, 'Billy-o! Mary-o! etc'.

Oanee iffee attoo: Only if he had to.

Obligin(g): Self-evident, but very much used locally, as in, 'I like gettin(g) my goods in that shop – very obligin(g) they are!'

Obstropalus: Preferred Wenglish pronunciation for 'obstreperous'.

Off!: Very angry, as in, 'Deuce, 'e was off! 'E din 'alf let 'em 'ave it!'

Off non: Off and on.

Offices: A word used in schooldays to describe school lavatories.

Off 'is 'ead: Taking leave of one's senses; 'Few-ree-uss (furious) 'e was when 'e saw it – I thought 'e was goin' off 'is 'ead fra minute!!' 'Off the deep end' is used also in this context.

O gow on!: Oh go on!

Old: A very interesting example of word usage since the word 'old' is frequently used to imply faint or positive disapproval in statements like '… making a lot of old fuss about nothing!' or '… only old enjoying themselves they think about these days!'

One: A 'case', a 'scream', a real character as in, 'E's a one! Never know what 'e'll come out with next!'

Once-over: A quick, but searching glance; I gave it the once-over but I decided it didn't need doing this time .'

On my (h)ands and knees: Begging, imploring (metaphorically): 'On my 'ands and knees I was to 'em – but they wouldn't listen a bit to me!'

On stop: Stopped, as in, 'Oh, 'e started off grand, but now, this week – it's all on stop with 'im!'

Only for: But for; 'Had a lovely time, we did – only for the rain, a coarse! '(of course)

Oo off? From whom? 'Oo off did you 'ave that then?'

Oose-pipe: Preferred local pronunciation of 'hose-pipe'.

Operatta: This is what an 'operetta' is often called locally.

Or loze: All those.

Out: Outside; 'Is it raining out? 'What is it like out today?'

Out, out: The double use echoes the Welsh way of expressing the same sort of thing to mean 'constantly' or 'all the time', as in, 'She's out, out, every day – always on the road, she is!' The opposite 'in, in' is used similarly to equal effect.

Over: It is prevalent in local speech to use 'over' to mean 'to', as in, 'I'm off over the Co-op' or, in Abercynon, where the river Cynon roughly bisects the village, 'I'm off over the other side!'

P

Pappish/Paps/Papsy: Very easy; 'The test we had today was paps.'

Paralatic: Seriously inebriated, as in "'E been comin 'ome paralatic from the 'Collier's' every Saturday night now frages, an' I tell you, gul, I really dunno jest 'ow much more of it I cun take.'

Pass the time of day: To pause and exchange greetings in a socially desirable way; 'He couldn't even be bothered to pass the time of day with me.'

Passin(g) remarks: Making (usually unfavourable) comments; 'Makes me sick, she do – always passin(g) remarks about somethin(g) or other'.

Penstiff: Stubborn. 'It's no use talking to him – a real penstiff, he is.'

Photos: The name given to fondly-remembered games with cigarette cards.

Picked up with: Got into company with, as in, 'There were some lovely people on holiday with us; we picked up with a couple from Manchester.'

Picky with food: Choosy and not easy to feed, as in, 'You got to be careful what you put in front of 'er – reeal picky with 'er food, she is.'

Pic-chers/Pictures/Pitchers: The local film show of days gone by; 'She's off to the pic-chers – first 'ouse!'

Piggies/Pickies: Trouble, as in, 'In the pickies proper 'e is now!'

Pimper: Pimping is the local word to describe the act of spying on courting couples. Those reprobates who crawled around the mountain-sides to watch the courting couples were called 'pimpers'.

Pisio/Pisho lawr: Used to describe very heavy rain by some older locals.

Pity (h)elp!: Used to show great sympathy for someone; 'Pity 'elp 'er, she'll 'ave 'er work cut out from now on …'

Play (h)ell: To make a great fuss and to carry on about something; 'Played 'ell about it, 'e did! – 'e 'ad 'is air off proper; now we'll never 'ear the end of it!'

Play the game: Behave fairly, as in, 'Thass nor (that's not) good enough – play the game, carn yue?' (can't you?)

Please, Mammy do ask: Remembered with affection from childhood – 'Please, Mammy do ask – can you come and see her after?'

Poinin(g)/Poenin(g): Troubling, as in Wenglish of yesteryear; 'Stop poinin(g) me will you? Can't you see I'm up to my eyes?' Probably from the Welsh word 'poeni' – to worry, pain or tease.

Pooer/poor look out: Poor prospects, as in, 'Pooer look out it'll be for them in there when she've gone.'

Pooer one: Not very adept; 'I'm a pooer one for Welshcakes but I can manidge (manage) pikeluts grand.'

Positive/Poz-tiv: Certain, as in, 'I'm positive it was him I saw down in Cardiff!'

Pot of sêm/saim: In a mess, in trouble; 'A real pot of sêm we were in with all them coming and the place not finished!' 'Saim' is the Welsh word for 'grease'.

Proper: Truly, really, as in, 'Proper fix I was in – cakes to make, out of flour, and every shop shut!'

Provoke: Annoy, as in, 'Stop youer provokin(g) will you – you're getting on everybody's nerves!'

Pudding rice/Pwdin reis: How rice pudding was named by older locals in days gone by, following the word order in Welsh.

Pull: Used to describe so many ailments that medical acquaintances (not from round here) tell me it is the cause of much confusion during consultations. Patients tell them they've had a pull, with almost every part of the anatomy!

Put myself straight: Put myself tidy, as in, 'I cleaned right through then I had to put myself straight before I went out.'

Put oneself: Used to describe confusion resulting from embarrassment – 'I didn't know where to put myself, really, when he said that!'

Put that safe! Put that in a safe place as in, '… an' make shuer you put that safe – there's no more where that came from!'

Pwdied/Poodied: Sulked, as in, 'She pwdied when we got back because we didn't tell her we were going.' 'Pwdu' is the Welsh word for 'to sulk or pout'.

Pylesa: Wenglish for 'piles of', similar to ' 'eapsa' for 'heaps of' and 'bagsa' for 'bags of'.

Q

Quite aware: The somewhat frosty reply from someone who may consider that you think that they have failed to grasp an implication or meaning; 'I'm quite aware of that, thank you!'

Quite a few: A fair number, as in, 'There was quite a few there this time.' 'Quite a few' and 'a tidy few' are probably used equally in Wenglish.

Quite a-willin(g): The addition of 'a' is seen again, as in 'not a-willing'. 'She's quite a-willin(g) as long as we get back before it's late.'

Quizzy: A Wenglish abbreviation for 'inquisitive'.

R

Racks jibidaires/jibidaires: An expression, meaning chaotic/in shambles/in rags and tatters/disintegrated, once heard frequently in 'Western Wenglish' areas. 'Rhacs is a Welsh word for 'rags' and 'ribidires' means 'rigmarole'. One wonders if 'rhibidires' became 'jibidires' via the same process as is seen at work, when it is recalled how 'rasper' and 'jasper' are often used inter-changeably in Wenglish.

Radically wrong: A much-used saying meaning 'very wrong'; 'There's something radically wrong with that kid of theyers – it's time they 'ad 'im seen to!'

Ranting and raving: Making a great deal of fuss, as in, 'Pay no attention to 'im, gul – 'e's always rantin' and ravin' about somethin' or other!'

Reeal bard: Seriously wrong or ill; 'I know 'e do make a fuss about everythin' 'e do 'ave, but 'e's reeal bard this time, for shuer!'

Relations: The preferred term locally for 'relatives', as in, 'All his relations are coming to the wedding.'

Riddle/riddler: The sieve used to separate small coal from lumps. The very small lumps thus separated are known as either as 'riddlings' or – more usually – 'ribblings'.

Right off: (1) Immediately; '... fairplay, 'e did it for me right off!'

(2) Having lost a liking for, as in, 'I'm right off pikelutts (pikelets), these days'.

Right through: Everywhere, completely, as in, 'That's the second time this week I've had to clean right through the house!'

Right you are then: A local expression showing firm agreement.

Ripe: Worn very thin; 'I'll afto get some new sheets – them I've got on the bed are proper ripe!'

Roaring laughing: Wenglish for laughing very heartily. An alternative is 'cracking laughing'.

Rose: The translation from the Welsh 'codi' – 'to rise' has led to a number of local uses for the word 'rose'. 'I rose my pension' or 'I rose some money from the bank' or 'They rose 'eaps a money for charity' or 'The funeral rose from the house, not from the chapel of rest' or 'When they all came in, I rose the dinner.'

S

Savin(g) (very): Thrifty; 'Very savin' she is – she's a good one to handle the money.'

Say: This provides a good example of the reversal of word order, as in, 'Your mother's askin, say ...'

Scatty: (1) Very fond of; 'Scatty for pink, she is! Always wears it every time!'

(2) 'Round the bend'; 'Driving me scatty, this weather is!'

Screws (the): Often used for 'rheumatics'. 'E' do get the screws terrible when the weather's like this.'

Scetting/Sketting (with rain): An expression used in some (western) parts for 'spitting', intermittent rain.

Scoot/Scwt!: (1) Be off!, Clear off! 'Scoot, will you – that's enough!'

(2) An expression which I have never heard, but which (I am assured) is used elsewhere in valley communities) to mean 'take the side of'; 'Don't worry now, I'll scoot for you!'

Scramcat: A girl who scrammed (scratched) when quarrelling.

Scrudge/Scrooge: Sweet and often sticky cake or dessert; I can't a-bear this old scrudge she puts in front of me.'

Scrumps/scrumpies: The broken off pieces of batter in the 'chip-shop'.

See you now, after: Another example of how, in Wenglish, 'now' seldom means 'immediately'.

Serviceable: Suiting the purpose ideally, as in, '… and it's very serviceable too – and it washes like a rag.'

Sglein: A surviving Welsh word for 'sparkle'; 'There's nice she do keep it – and there's a sglein on it all …'

Shapin(g): Coming along well, as in, ''E 'ad a lot of potch with it, but its shaping with 'im now…'

Shark: Cheat, as in the old Wenglish expression, 'Don't shark the gwt!' (Don't cheat the queue!).

Shift your stumps: Wenglish for 'move yourself'

Shinkyn/Shenkyn: A once popular drink of sweet tea in a basin with pieces of bread in it (and sometimes eaten with cheese).

Shoes full of my feet; An apt description for swollen feet after a long period of walking or standing.

Shoutin(g) an(d) bawlin(g): Noisily reacting: 'Take no notice of 'im – 'e's always shoutin' and bawlin' 'bout somethin' or other!'

Sickener (had a): Had a sickening of, as in, 'I've 'ad a proper sick'ner of all them cowboy films on the telly!'

Sioni Oy: A variation of 'Sioni Dai' for someone whose appearance leaves much to be desired.

Sketch: An untidy or a somewhat bizarre appearance, as in, 'Doesn't she look a sketch in that rig-out she's got on?!'

Skimpy: Less than adequate.

Skinful (had a): Drunk – or very nearly so, as in, ''e' won't be 'ome from the club till 'e's 'ad a skinful, you can bet!'

Skinny ribs: What thin persons were once called locally.

Slipped up: Erred, as in, 'You slipped up there – you should have asked him while he was in a good mood.'

Slippin(g) (you're): Not as good as you once were; 'You're slippin(g)! I can remember the time you'd have done that by now!'

Slong 'en: Wenglish for 'So long, then'

Slummocky/Sloch: Untidy, as in, 'Let 'erself go, she 'ave – gone to look proper slummocky, she is!' A person who is constantly 'slummocky' may well be called a 'sloch'.

Smack in the chops: A (metaphorical) blow to one's hopes; ' 'ad a reeal smack in the chops, she did, when she found out the truth!'

Smooth/Smoothio: The old Welsh-influenced word for 'ironing'.

Soft-soapin(g): Trying to 'get around' someone, as in, 'It's no use you tryin' youer soft-soapin' on me – I've met youer sort before …'

Spanish: The word from childhood, for 'liquorice', pronounced 'Spar-nish'.

Sparkin(g): Old Wenglish word for 'courting'.

Sponar: Another old Wenglish word, this time meaning 'girl-friend' (does the word 'spooner' have something to do with it?)

Square up: (1) To settle up, as in, 'I had to square up with 'im before 'e went.'

(2) To make tidy, as in, 'I'll have to square up before I go out.'

Stamp: Build; 'Look at them two – the boy's the same stamp as his dad, exactly.'

State: Condition, as in, 'Look at the state this place is in – you ought to be ashamed of youerself!'

Stex/Stecks/Sticks: A sticky mess, like a baby's used bib, or used to describe anything in a soiled condition; 'We'll afto do somethin' about this place – there's sticks and stecks everywhere!!'

Stillions: A hand-held, weighing device.

Stir your stumps: See 'shift your stumps'.

Stomp/Stump: Another local name for the mixture of potato and swede, otherwise called 'potch'.

Stoning the flags/doorstep: The way in which stone floors and doorsteps were once cleaned locally.

Stripped off to half: Having all one's upper clothing removed – posibly ready to have 'a tidy swill'.

Supter yue: Wenglish for 'it's up to you'.

Sure to be: Certainly, as in, 'You'll find six at least there – sure to be' This is a direct translation of the Welsh 'siwr o fod'.

Swill through: To wash out by hand; 'It's a bit stecky, I'd better give it a quick swill through to freshen it up.'

Swindle: Popular local word for a sweepstake or raffle.

Swizz: A 'swindle' or a 'con-trick'; 'It's a big swizz, innit? – saying there was things to be 'ad there for nothin'!'

Swole up: Swollen, as in, ''E' ad this bard arm an' then, they rushed 'im into 'ospital cos it all swole up with 'im.'

Squint: A quick look; 'Let's have a squint then – don't keep it cwtched.'

T

Tafod teg: A smooth talker; The Welsh expression literally means 'a fair tongue'; 'Don't trust him, will you? – proper old tafod teg he is!'

Talking nineteen to the dozen: Talking a great deal and getting it out very fast.

Talu' fory: This Welsh expression (meaning 'pay tomorrow') was once much-used to describe hire-purchase payments.

Tanner to raise the latch: Sixpence to start off an evening's drinking session in the hope that others would provide later.

Telling lies like talking Welsh: Once used locally to describe an accomplished liar.

Terrible/Terruble: Badly affected, as in, 'She've 'ad this terrible leg/chest etc. this ages.' An alternative is to say, 'She've 'ad a terrible time with 'er leg/chest/etc ...'

Thar way: Wenglish for 'that way'.

Thasserfack: Wenglish for 'that's a fact'.

Thasser good 'un/That's a good one: 'Tell me another!' as in, 'That's a good one – you'll paint the outside! You haven't finished the kitchen yet!'

Thass gowin: That's going, as in, 'He's the biggest liar thass gowin, that one!'

Thass typical: That's just like; 'Thass typical of you that is – all promises!' The alternative is often 'Thass you all over, that is!'

The lorravum/lorrovue: Wenglish for 'the lot of them/you'. 'Now, buzz off the lorrovue before I give one of you a clout!'

There you are then: A satisfactory conclusion is often rounded off with these words which are a translation of the Welsh form.

There's … for you! The habit of tagging on 'for you' to statements like 'There's lovely for you!' or 'there's posh for you!' is the result of direct translation of the Welsh 'dyna … i ti/chi/chwi'.

This long time: For a long time; 'We been selling these things this long time'. This is an acceptable alternative to 'this ages' and 'frages'.

This years: For a long time. 'This years', 'this long time', and 'this ages'/'issages' are all used interchangeably to express the same meaning in Wenglish.

Thought sure: Was firmly convinced, as in, 'I thought sure he'd be here by now, but there's no sign of him anywhere.'

Tiddly bit: The old name for that old coin, the silver threepenny bit.

Tight: In local usage, this means both 'drunk' and 'mean'.

Tipped the wink: Signalled the appropriate time, as in, 'When I was ready to go, I tipped 'im the wink'.

Tipping down: Raining very heavily.

Titchy: Small as in, 'Titchy little feller 'e is – make two of 'im she would!'

Tod-end: Wenglish for a cigarette stub; also 'dog-end' or 'nip'.

Toe the line: Conform to the rules, as in, 'Just you wait, my lady – you'll have to toe the line when your father comes back!'

Too short to cut cabbage: Saying applied to the shorter than average in the land of fairly short people.

Too tired to get out of his own way: An often-heard local saying; 'Lazy's not the word for 'im – 'e's too tired to get out of 'is own way!'

Toot (on my): On my nerves, as in, '… get on my toot, 'e do, with all 'is old nonsunse.' (nonsense).

Told straight: Told without possibility of misunderstanding, as in, 'I was fed up with it – and I told her straight!'

To tell the trueth (truth): 'Truth to tell' in local speech.

Touch and go, it was: Self-evident, but the word-order gives the Wenglish flavour; 'Touch and go, it was – thought we'd lost 'im that time, pooer dab!'

Travel the side/back: A local injunction to use the side/back entry to a house.

Trood; In Wenglish, this is the past tense of 'tread'; 'She've gone to clean 'er shoes 'cos she trood in something out there!'

Turned round: Followed up with, as in, '… an' then what do you think 'e turned round and said/did?'

Turned spiteful: Become unhelpful/unco-operative, as in, 'She turned spiteful on me when I wouldn't give 'er a lend of it.'

Twndish: An old Wenglish word for a small funnel.

Twpsan: A female who is 'twp', i.e. a bit slow on the uptake.

Twpsyn/Twpsan dwl: Someone who is very stupid.

Tylwyth/Tylwth: The Welsh for 'family' or 'tribe', as in, 'I carn a-bear goin' when 'er hool (whole) tylwth's there.'

U

Uh? Widely used in local parts for 'pardon?'

Under a specialist as well as the doctor: A measure of 'poshness' as well as an example of 'one-upmanship'.

Up and downer: A blazing row; a violent argument; 'They had a real up and downer about her staying out late again.'

Up England way: Generally used to refer to any geographical location more or less east of Newport (Gwent). Used delightfully vaguely as in, 'You know where they've gone to live, gul – up England way, somewhere!'

'urdy-gurdy: The name given by some to any gadget whose name has temporarily been forgotten!

V

Venter: Assume, wager, as in, 'You can venter it was him who put them up to it!' 'Mentro' (one of whose mutated forms is 'fentro', pronounced 'ventro') is the Welsh for 'venture'.

W

Wears ee to?/Where's he to? Wenglish for 'Where is he?'

Wedjan: Old Wenglish word for 'a girl friend'. I am told that husbands often spoke of their wives as 'y wedjan'.

Well away: (1) Prosperous, as in, 'Well away 'e is now – got a tidy bit in the bank, I know!'

(2) Drunk; 'After a night out with 'is mates, 'e was well away when 'e rolled 'ome 'ere!'

Went: Developed/became so that, as in, 'She went, she wouldn't eat/talk/take notice etc. etc. …'

Went flying: Fell very heavily; 'Went flying, she did - she've 'urt 'erself reeal bard this time!'

What's the onions/carrots/apples/oranges?: A Wenglish form of enquiring the price of various commodities; 'What's the onions with you today?'

What (are) you on about? What are you talking about, as in, 'What you on about now? We settled that last week.'

What's up?/Wossup?: What is the matter? as in, 'Wossup with you *this* time? You're never satisfied unless you're cribbin' about somethin' or other!'

When it came to: When matters reached fruition, as in, '… promised faithful, 'e did – but when it came to, no sign of 'im!'

Wisp: The preferred local word for sty or stye, the eye infection. Although I was fortunate never to have suffered from one of these, I recall the passing of wedding rings over the wisp (I am told that coins were used for this purpose, too) and being sent to bring spring water to bathe the eyes of other members of the family who suffered from 'wisps'.

With his/her: Because of, as in, 'He's under the doctor with his nerves/legs/chest' etc.

With you: At your home, as in, 'Keep it all nice, you do – always looks lovely with you!'

With your finger in your mouth: Not having enough money, as in, 'If you're going on that outing, you better save your money – you can't go there with your finger in your mouth!'

Wodger won now? Wenglish for 'What do you want now?'

Woonshee? Wenglish for 'Won't she?'

Work cut out: Given a hard task; hard put to; 'Say what you do like – they'll 'ave theyr work cut out tryin' to get 'im to alter 'is stroke!'

Worrue after now? Wenglish for 'what are you after now?'

Wouldn't give it (h)ouse room: A popular local expression showing firm unwillingness to have anything to do with something.

Won't know youerself/himself/herself, etc. A local saying to show how great will be the improvement, as in, 'When she moves to one of them flats, she won't know herself, after battling with all those old stairs all these years!'

Wrgi: A man noted for his sexual prowess in former times; the literal meaning seems to be 'a male dog'. 'You want to watch him – he's an old wrgi!'

Items of 'News in Wenglish'

Similar to those broadcast on Radio Wales

These items are given first in Standard English, then in their Wenglish 'translations'.

I once saw this report in the *South Wales Echo:*

A senior medical practitioner has warned that more and more doctors are suffering from such stress that they end up hating their patients. He further said that it is vital that patients should take more care of their doctors. Patients can help greatly by telling their doctor how grateful they are for his attention to their ailments. They can also help by spotting tell-tale signs, such as being abrupt and dismissive of patients' views, cancelling appointments, and smelling of strong drink. Being observant and having consideration for doctors will help considerably and will ensure that doctors do not become overwought.

Wenglish:

I came across this bit in the *'Echoo'* nosso long back:

Accordin' to one a them 'igh-up doctors, 'eaps an' 'eaps a doctors are gerrin in a proper state an' do get to the point where they 'ave gone, they 'ate theyer payshunts. 'E went on to say that iss crueshul that payshunts should keep an eye reg'lar on theyer doctors. Payshunts cun 'elp a grate deal by tellin' the doctor theyer reelly grateful for 'im seein' to theyer complaints. Payshunts cun also lend 'and by keepin' theyer eye out for them signs which do give the show away; like this, they are: bein' awful short-tempered, not payin' attenshun or listenin' tidy to what payshunts do tell 'em, not bein' there when 'e'd promised faithful, an' stinkin' somethin' chronic a beer an' whisky. Watchin' points an' 'avin a think about 'ow the doctor might be feelin' a bit rough now an' agen, will 'elp 'eaps an' make shuer that the doctor don' work 'imself up into a reeal frazzle.

$\cdot$ $\cdot$ $\cdot$

This item deals with a woman talking about things in general and the problems of life in particular:

'I was in trouble intending to make a quick and simply-made cake for tea and then finding I had no flour. The shops were closed early for the half-day, so I didn't know what to do. I couldn't ask my neighbour because she's so unreliable and I wouldn't expect any sense from her. By the time I'd seen my friend off on the bus (and she missed it, anyway) and tidied myself up, it was too late to go shopping in Ponty. My daughter saved the situation: she brought me some Welshcakes and drop scones she had baked especially for me.'

Wenglish:

'I was in a proper fix; I was goin' to make some *teisen lap* for our tea and I found I was right out a flour with none to be 'ad because the shops was shut, early closin'. I din know where to turn. I couldn't ask 'er next door 'cos there's no depends on 'er an' she's a bit of a flag. Against I'd sent my friend on the bus (an' she lost it, in any case) an' put myself straight, there was the time, gone, an' every shop shut in Ponty. My daughter saved my bacon, she brought me some pics and some pikeluts she'd done for me special.'

.   .   .

Two men were having a discussion about one of their friends and his wife. 'She's such a gasbag', said one, she goes all over the town talking about everyone and carrying tales. And what a loud voice she has! You can't mistake her screeching! She's always keeping on at him and he can't get a word in edgeways. He's henpecked, without a doubt. She's well-built, tall, and twice his size! If he gave her any cheek, she'd certainly floor him. I'm very sorry for him, but it's of no use trying to change him, or there would be an almighty row, and she would make life unbearable for him. She's a virago, without doubt.'

Wenglish

A couple of fellers was 'avin' a chinwag about one a theyer butties an' 'is missis. 'She's a proper chopsy one,' said one of 'em. 'She's all over the place carryin' on about somebody or other nineteen to the dozen an' carrying clecs. An' she've got a bell on every tooth! There's no mistakin' that screch of 'ers! Always pickin' on 'im, she is an' 'e carn gerra word in to save 'is life. *She* do wear the trousers, for shuer, she's a reeal boilin piece an' a fair 'ighth – make two of 'im she would! If 'e gave 'er any lip, she'd give 'im a reeal fetcher! I'm sorry my 'eart frim, but it's no good tryin' to alter 'is stroke, 'cos there'd be ructions an' she'd give 'im 'ell. She's a proper sprateus – an' thass for shuer.'

.   .   .

Aesop's fable of *The Ant and the Grasshopper* retold in Wenglish.

All through the long 'ot summer and the autumn, a little ant 'ad ben 'ard at it, makin' shuer 'e 'ad 'eaps of food frimself an' 'is fam'ly before the winter. Day after day 'e was back an' fore, back an' fore to 'is cwtch an' 'e din even stop to take a wiff – oany when 'e atto, until 'e was positive 'e 'ad plenty to see 'im through when the snow an' ice was about, an' there wouldn't be a 'aputh a food to be 'ad.

One mornin', in the middle a winter – an' a sharp one it was – that little ant was luggin' out some a the corn 'e'd put by, 'cos 'e wanted to gerrit dried out tidy, ready to eat, like … Who should come on to 'im then but a titchy, 'ungry grass'opper an' 'e begged the ant for some of 'is food, 'cos 'e was famished like, - starvin' 'e was, you could tell straight off. 'Oany a eyeful, I want', 'e said, 'I 'aven't gorra bit a food to my name'.

'What was you up to in the summer, like?' said the ant, 'there was loadsa food to be 'ad then – the 'ool place was *full* a food, there for the takin', all through them long, 'ot days a summer, so there was plenty a stuff for you to make a cwtch to keep it in, innit?'

'Well,' said the grass'opper, 'I don't want you to think fra minute that I was 'alf-soaked, like; I was 'ard at it – everyday reg'lar I was out an' about.'

'Well, what was you doin' then?' said the ant – askin 'im straight, like.

'From first go off in the mornin' till last lap in the night, I was singin' reeal belfago – 'ere, there an' everywhere, I was – ask anybody round 'ere!'

But the ant 'ad no patience with 'im at all an' 'e thought to 'imself that this grass'opper must be a bit of a flag an' twp as a sledge to carry on that shape'. 'Well,' 'e said, as 'e was shuttin the door to 'is cwtch where 'is food was all piled up, tidy, 'If you can sing all summer, you can dance all winter – so there frue!' An' 'e shut the cwtch door sharpish. 'Ard –'earted that ant was! 'There's mingy!' did I 'ear somebody say? Well praps, praps indeed … but when yue stop an' think about it fra spell, you gorrw admit this stoary *do* 'ave a lesson frall of us to 'ave a think about innit? You gorrw keep 'ard at it an' take care to put by plenty a what you goin' to need later on … 'cos, honest, now – you carn expect to go cap in 'and to somebody else all a time, an' get 'em to 'elp you out now, cun yue? – wara-teg, like!

David and Goliath

The children of Israel was in a real pot o' sêm; there was this big, 'uge feller called Goliath – one of them Philerstines 'e was, see, an' every day 'e was paradin' back an' fore, back an' fore in front a the Israelite camp an' callin' 'em rotten for being cowards, 'cos they wouldn't choose one of 'em to come out an' fight 'im tidy!

But 'e was a reeal giunt, like, built like the side of 'ouse, 'e was – so yue carn blame them Israelites for bein' backward in comin' forwud, cun yue? One day, David's dad, Jesse, 'ad asked 'im to take some things for David's older brothers who was in the army, an' 'e said, 'Find out 'ow theyer gerrin on an' let me know, will yue?'

'Right-you-are', said David, an' off 'e went.

When David reached the camp 'e could 'ear a lor a palaver with this bloke Goliath goin' on at them Israelites an' tellin' 'em what a lot of cowards they was – proper blaggud 'e was, yue could tell, like see. David went straight off to the king – Saul 'is name was – an' 'e said, 'Lemme 'ave a go at this Goliath feller!'

Saul warn a bit willin' first go off, 'I carn 'ave a crot like yue up against this giunt, cun I?'

But David kept on an' on about it an' said 'e could manidge fine; so in the end, Saul atto give in to 'im, an' 'e manidged to fix David up with a 'elmet, a coat a mail, an' a reeal bomper of a sword – went the 'ool 'og 'e did!! When David tried all these things on, 'e couldn't budge, an' 'e said to Saul straight, 'There's no shape like this – I carn fight tidy with this lot!'

So they atto take 'em off 'im agen. David took 'is big stick, chose five smooth pebbles out the stream an' 'e put 'em in 'is shepherd's barg. 'This is more my dap,' said David, an' then, with 'is sling in 'is 'and, off 'e went to fight Goliath.

When Goliath saw David 'e was laughin' fittobust. 'Come over by 'ere,' 'e said, an' I'll give yue a *reeal* lambastin; an' last go off, I'll feed youer flesh to the birds an' animals round 'ere!'

David warn put off a bit by all this carryin' on. 'Today,' 'e said, proud like, 'Today, God will let me put one over on yue – you'll see now jest what I do mean!'

'I'm on a good thing 'ere,' thought the giant, an' up 'e came, full fuss, to put David in 'is place, once an' frall! David was all there, mind, an' 'e put 'is 'and in 'is barg an' took out a pebble, put it in 'is sling, an' then, like a winky, 'e aimed it right at Goliath's forrid. An' Goliath fell down - *crash!!* 'cos thar pebble 'ad gone right into 'is forrid, an' 'e was dead before 'e even touched the ground!

When them Philerstines saw what 'ad 'appened to theyer champion, they din' 'ang about to see what would 'appen next – they was off, with the Israelites aftrum, yellin' blue murder!

Saul was thrilled to bits with David, an' 'e took a reeal fancy to 'im, an' 'e said, from that day on, 'e was to come an' live with 'im an' all 'is family, an' be like one of 'is own boys.

So, from then on, yue could say, David the shepherd boy was landed, warn 'e?'

1. He'll be a tidy spell, I expect.
2. Because they was bard, they stayed home after all.
3. … and he had the cheek to say it isn't his fault at all.
4. We've been on to them about it this ages, but it's no use.
5. Why didn't he say? He only had to mention it to me.
6. It's all according to what he'll say, really.
7. Keep your eye out for one of them.
8. You'll see now just what will happen to them.
9. Don't she have a lot of potch with them?
10. Where the hell has he gone now, do you suppose?
11. He hasn't been this long time, but he said he would.
12. Shopping down the precinct? I'm not fussed, really!
13. That's a fact? You've got to be joking!
14. She didn't know which way to turn for him half the time.
15. Enough's enough, I do say to them.
16. They were (was) all there, bar (except) one of them.
17. Still undecided they are about going.
18. There are times I could cry, if I stopped to think.
19. Get those (them) clothes off the line, it's coming on to rain.
20. Don't keep on, will you? There's none for you this time.
21. She carried it in her handbag.
22. He's after something or other all the time these days.
23. What's the time by you? When is stop-tap?
24. Keep an eye on that, I've got to slip out for a spell.
25. Give us it here or you'll cop it!
26. Have you had a tidy swill? Let me see your hands.
27. He's trying to figure out who did it to him.
28. Piles of them are coming if they can have the day off.
29. Will you be down the club later on, or no?
30. He'll have to leave it go because he's getting on a bit now.
31. Awful one, he is, for his pikelets.
32. The length of his tongue was all she had in the end!
33. If you don't watch it, you'll get a damned good hammering!
34. No shape on him round the house – proper ham-fisted, he is!
35. If you don't heisht (be quiet), and stop all that grizzling, I'll give you what for!
36. There's times I do wonder is it worth it!
37. Happy to see the back of them she'll be, right enough!
38. So long, then, see you after – (are) you coming to our house or me up yours?
39. We'll have to come to some arrangement later on, I expect.
40. As a matter of fact, he's gone the whole hog this time!
41. Let (loose) go, will you? That's mine, not yours!
42. She's gone down what's-her-name's and then she's off to see what-do-you-call.
43. I've had about all I can take this time!

44. Chopsy one and full of clecs (tales), he was, but I soon choked him off!
45. If I don't see to it straight away (off), it's no use at all.
46. Patient he was, love him!
47. Pity help us if he takes over, if that's all he can do about it!
48. Hopeless he is, he hasn't got a clue!
49. Keep yourself tidy for a spell till (clean until) they arrive here.
50. Married? Never! Living tally (together) they are, right enough!
51. He's afraid he'll have to have it done again.
52. We're off for holidays now in a couple of months.
53. Boy-and–a-half, he is – he had us laughing fit to bust.
54. Quite willing she was, in the end, to have it done for her.
55. Why does he keep on about it when he knows he's in the wrong?
56. Had to have a bit of a whiff (breather), he did, because he was out of puff.
57. In the end, it got so bad they had to have it seen to.
58. I'll have it again, if that's all right.
59. If I didn't now differently, I'd reckon he's not all there half the time.
60. While he was there, he had his hair cut as well.
61. There's not much else here now like, is there really?

Answers to advanced examples:

1. He's been going now, on and off, back and forth, for ages, but it hasn't done him all that much good I reckon.
2. That's all he said about it, but if he did – tamping mad she was, and keeping on the whole time he was there.
3. We're having somebody in for the papering, then he'll have to get on with the emulsioning.
4. He's got it in his head that he's a real cert. for it, but he hasn't got a hope in hell as I see it.
5. How's he off for sticks these days now he's given up working down the pit?
6. I've got to admit I do feel heaps better these days, better than I've been this ages, I suppose.
7. Went off the deep end, he did, like as if he had to, he can't help himself when he do have one of his bouts!
8. Potching about he was, instead of doing it tidy as he was supposed to, but it's no use keeping on to him!
9. If he'd only listen! But I might as well give it up as a bad job for all he do care about it.
10. He's had a lot of potch trying to get some clothes to suit him, but he's fixed up now.
11. He's got on famous really, he's got a lot of men under him at work.
12. All right then, have it your own way, but if it was up to me, I'd show them a thing or two, that's all I got to say.

John Edwards undertook many after-dinner engagements illustrating the art of speaking Wenglish.

'Wenglish' CDs featuring John Edwards with live audiences are also available:

'Wenglish Revised'

'The Best of Wenglish' Volume 1

'The Best of Wenglish' Volume 2

'Wenglish Stories'

All are available from:

Black Mountain Records
1 Squire Court
The Marina
Swansea SA1 3XB

Telephone 01792 301500

Publisher's footnote: Tidy people everywhere should agree and fervently hope that John Edward's timeless little classics shall *never again* disappear from the shelves!